**How weird can it get?**

**Andrew Jones**

Sonedge Inc
P.O. Box 8490
Kingston CSO
Jamaica, W.I.

© Andrew Jones
First published in 2009

All rights reserved. No part of this publication may be reproduced, stored in a retrieval system or transmitted in any form or in any means, electronic, mechanical, photo-copying, recording or otherwise, without the prior permission of the publishers.

Front Cover and Back Cover designs: Photographed by Andrew Jones of a wooded scene at a rural high school in Jamaica.

The author wishes to state that the views are his.

This book was published in 2009, and reprinted in 2011.

Manufactured in Jamaica, West Indies
Sonedge Inc.
P.O. Box 8490
Kingston CSO
Jamaica, W.I.

ISBN 978-976-610-843-4

# Contents

| | |
|---|---|
| Family Ties | 5 |
| The legacy of the AJ - pioneering activities | 16 |
| What makes the AJ different from everyone else? | 25 |
| The AJ - the source of controversy | 29 |
| Dealing with love and its challenges - as a teenager | 39 |
| Dealing with love and its challenges - as an adult | 49 |
| The AJ - simmering like a meal cooking in a pot | 59 |

To

My ex-dearest:
While having many conversations with her, she often said, "Why don't you write a book?" Well my ex-dearest, your wish has been granted. Enjoy reading this book, ok?

My 'puddytat' daughter:
This book was written in part to inform her of the legacy that she might not know about- without reading some of these brief recollections of events that her father was involved in - as well as perhaps, she may benefit from the proceeds of this publication.

## Family ties

The AJ was born in a nuclear family comprising of the typical parents and siblings, in March 1962. His parents not only decided to cohabit in the same house- each with differing backgrounds and life experiences, had older children of their own- but were unmarried to each other and had very little material wealth at their disposal. Could you imagine the struggle for this couple, when it was known that another baby (yours truly) shall be born to them?

The AJ recalled with joy and some sadness, aspects of his early childhood; which was supported by family pictures, comments by his siblings and rants by his mother. For example, the AJ remembered receiving and riding his first tricycle which was either for his fourth or fifth birthday gift from his father. The AJ remembered of this occasion that he used the tricycle as a ladder to practice painting a wall of his dad's house to his peril. As soon as the AJ attempted to balance himself on the handle of the tricycle, shortly afterwards he not only fell off the handle; bruising his chin, hands and knees, but he was also doused by the pail of water that used as the imaginary paint.

The AJ also remembered that as early as he could recall as

a child, he was chastised by my mother for doing things 'like his father', and resembling him too! Ooh, on a different note, as a six year old child, the AJ had very good artistic skills. He remembered being praised for drawing a real life image of a lion, with this drawing being put on display at his basic school 'art board' at the time.

Unfortunately, the AJ's parents separated from each other, as his mother moved out of his dad's house with the children (his siblings and him), when he was about seven years old. Of course, that event created many challenges for the AJ; as he was ultimately thrown further into the middle of his parental disputes, with some of those experiences were not pleasant to bear.

As time progressed, the AJ found out that growing up in this environment was challenging for himself and his siblings. Economic resources were fast depleting, and while the AJ's dad had a stable job, his mother (by virtue of her action to move out of his dad's house) had to find a job in order to at least support her newly formed female headed household comprising of six persons; mother, the AJ and his four siblings.

Despite, experiencing many family oriented challenges, the AJ said that he had a good childhood. In his opinion, the AJ stated that his parents did whatever they could to provide for him; with food, shelter and security, schooling and educational opportunities (including his participation in extra curricula activities), and religious teaching opportunities. The AJ continued to mention that his parents also provided him with 'guided' freedom to form friendships and associations with other humans, as well as the opportunities to learn how to live as a member of a civil society. The AJ expressed gratitude to them (his parents) for giving him the opportunity to be taught about the importance of developing strong family values; while introducing him to his extended family on a timely basis.

The AJ said that he experienced many great as well as weird moments while growing up as a child. Certainly, the AJ was embroiled in sibling rivalry, especially between his younger brothers and himself. Perhaps, one may say that these events should be classified as normal occurrences.

However, based on the edicts of the AJ's parents (mainly his mother), the impact of these sibling rivalry activities on them, the children were curtailed to a minimum. For example, the AJ and his siblings were not forced to compete for the use of toys, school books, bed space, clothing, love and attention, and even for physical space. Why? It was because all of the children were not only given their own toys, books, clothing and so on, but they were 'effectively' taught the importance of sharing (even when they have other opinions of the topic).

In addition, the AJ and his siblings knew that sanctions would be rigidly applied- should any of them decided otherwise. Of interest, the AJ commented that it was as a result of the actions like those mentioned above that were instrumental in his being grown up as an independent, self sufficient individual for the future.

On reflection on the many events that have impacted the AJ's childhood life, he often wondered how weird did some of those things get. The AJ hereby presented a list of some of his concerns in this regard. Firstly, based on his parents efforts at providing effective health care for the household, none of his siblings and he ever had a childhood disease whatsoever (such as the Measles, Chicken Pox, the Mumps, Lice infection etc). However, the AJ contracted the Mumps at age 27- while playing in one of his inter-office football competitions.

Secondly, it was expected that children above the age of 14 years old would be introduced to the world of work- by at getting at least a summer job. However, despite the fact that the economic resources of his mother's household were limited, neither the AJ nor his siblings ever had to get a job until after they completed their secondary education (Please note, it has not been suggested that getting a summer job was a bad thing to do, ok?).

Thirdly, the AJ and his siblings played almost every conceivable contact sport as children, yet none of them suffered a broken bone, or were hospitalized as a result of their involvement in those sports. Of interest, none of the children -that is, the AJ and his siblings- ever sustained any physical/psychological trauma that required special medical attention for an extended time after visiting a medical doctor for a routine medical check-up.

Fourthly, it was noted that 'teen age pregnancy' occurrences were prevalent in the community that the AJ lived in, yet neither his sisters nor his brothers experienced 'teen age pregnancy' situations themselves.

Fifthly, many of the AJ's childhood friends got into serious trouble with the legal authorities including the police. Despite his siblings and he being very close friends to these people, (i.e. their peers) they were never 'entangled' with the law. In fact, neither the AJ nor his siblings were ever detained, arrested and/or charged with any offence whatsoever, under the law.

Sixthly, while growing up as children, the AJ and his siblings never spent a holiday away from home –whether as a result of during any school summer break or any national holiday recognition.

Seventhly, despite knowing that at least one of the children of the household possessed 'noted' sporting skills and organizational aptitudes, the AJ was the only child who represented his school in any sporting/social/ academic endeavors.

Eight of all, the AJ and his siblings were discouraged from making friends with adults and their peers in the neighborhood. However, the AJ and his siblings seemed able to attract a large gathering of persons who enjoyed their company and became friends with them, (mainly secretively) often without their mother's consent / permission. Of note, whenever the AJ's mother had to be absent from home (such as when she had to go to work), many of the neighborhood's children often gravitated towards the yard to share the use of their toys with them (the AJ and his siblings); as many of these children did not have or own any toys to play with for themselves. Ooh, on the topic of sharing toys, later in this chapter the AJ promised to recall and share an incident with you that always cause him to smile.

Ninthly, the AJ and his siblings were discouraged from getting into fights. However, the AJ and one of his older sisters were deceptively good tactical fighters, especially the youngest of his older sisters C.P. Of course, the AJ's mother was never told of her exploits by the children.

Tenthly, in the community where the AJ and his siblings lived as children, they and their immediate neighbors' children were the oddities; in that, they collectively seemed to have escaped the trappings of poverty, apparently when they all 'boarded and rode the educational opportunity train'. None of them failed to achieve their reasonable academic objectives. In fact, all of these children mentioned earlier have become productive individuals in the society, based on their chosen career paths that they envisioned as children. Also, a feeling of accomplishment can be noted within the realm of the extended family of the AJ; as all of them have held dignified positions in life without getting 'entangled' by breaching the tenets of the law.

As mentioned earlier, on the topic of sharing toys, the AJ recalled a real life story that always caused him to smile. This story began as follows: The AJ received a 'piggy bank' for his tenth year birthday gift – in order to encourage him to develop the habit of being thrifty. He showed this gift to his friends, and the AJ eventually convinced them to adopt the idea of using his 'piggy bank' on display to save some of their pocket money in it.

The AJ, being the 'Banker', collected his friends' monies from them. He then made a receipt book; in order to record each individual's monetary allocation that he received for their collective savings accounts. At the end of each 'banking' day, the AJ would usually store the documents and the 'piggy bank' under the cellar of his house; so that he could avoid his mother discovering his activities.

On one of those fateful nights of the AJ's childhood banking career, the rains came. Unknowing to him, the flood waters from that overnight rain flowed under the house and washed away both the 'piggy bank' and the receipt book that he had.

In the morning following the overnight rain episode described earlier, the AJ recalled that one of his 'childhood bank' client friends visited him to retrieve some of his money. The AJ went to the spot under the cellar that he hid/placed the 'piggy bank' and the receipt book, only to find nothing. Subsequently, the AJ was given a nickname 'Tish it away' because the flood waters washed away the 'piggy bank' and his banking records. In addition to experiencing the financial losses as well as receiving a blow to his 'budding childhood banking career, the AJ had to refund monies to his friends; whatever they told him that they had deposited in his bank. Lessons learnt!

Having told the story as the AJ promised, let us return to the sequence of events at hand. As soon as the AJ became an adult, his role in the family structure changed dramatically; and he had to deal with the realities. For example, all his sisters had already left his mother's household - due to marriage and academic pursuits - and he (the AJ) was still being chastised for possessing attributes and personality traits of his father. In addition, the pressures of the his mother's life climaxed for the AJ when he was ejected from her household shortly after completing his secondary school education at age 19.

Luckily for the AJ, he was immediately accepted by his father to live with him (at his home). Incidentally, one of the AJ's younger brothers left their mother's household within 24 hours after he was ejected, to live with their dad and him.

The AJ recalled that he, having never spent a night at his father's home during either as a child or during his youth, got the opportunity to live with him for the first time permanently. This living arrangement between the AJ and his dad continued until he died (at about the same time that the AJ was setting up house with his eventual wife at the time.)

The AJ recalled that it was during that time of living with his father, that he found out that his father was (a) a powerful teacher of 'the ways of the world' and (b) a great storyteller- in explaining his pronouncements to him. The AJ confessed that as a result of being exposed to his father's instructions and personal behavior, not only impacted him positively, but it helped to mold him into the man that he became.

For example, the AJ said that his father told him a story – reinforcing the efforts of his mother at instilling positive values needed in his male siblings and him- to illustrate that they (as children) ought to avoid getting into trouble. This story according to the AJ began like this.

The AJ's father said that when he (the dad) was about nine years old, he enjoyed roaming the neighborhood that he lived in with his friends of a similar age group. In his neighborhood, there was a large acreage farm owner whose name was 'Harry' (for the purposes of this story). On this property, 'Harry' operated a mango orchard. During crop time, children usually frequent this farm illegally to pick and eat the mangoes. By the same token, 'Harry' often warned trespassers about the consequences of being caught on his farm without his permission.

In an attempt to prevent any trouble with this landowner, the parents of one of the AJ's dad childhood friends (say his name is 'Johnny') not only stripped him of all his clothing, but hid all the other items of clothing that 'Johnny' possessed. This was done to prevent 'Johnny' from roaming the neighborhood – and eventually ending up illegally visiting 'Harry's' farm with my dad and the other of their friends.

On that fateful day (according to the AJ father's story) when 'Johnny's clothing was taken from him, another of his dad's childhood friends visited him. He saw that 'Johnny' was naked, loaned him some of his own clothing so that they could join the other children and enjoy their usual activities together as a group.

As soon as they (the children) were all reunited, they went on their usual stroll in the neighborhood.

On approaching 'Harry's' farm, these children not only entered the mango orchard illegally, but 'Harry' hurriedly climbed up one of the mango trees, laden with ripe mangoes. 'Harry' began picking and eating mangoes, while simultaneously dropping ripe mangoes that he picked from the tree for the AJ's dad and his childhood friends to eat. The AJ's dad and his friends were so involved in the picking up and eating mangoes that they did not recognize that the owner - 'Harry' – had entrapped them.

'Harry' snuck out of his hiding place and pounced upon the children.

According to the AJ father's story, 'Johnny' was the only child caught by 'Harry', as all the other children (including the AJ's father) who were not in a tree, fled the scene. 'Harry' ordered 'Johnny' out of the tree, held him by the back of his pants and began dragging him off to the police station. In his initial shock, 'Johnny' tried to free himself from the grasp of 'Harry' while kicking and screaming for help.

During the journey, 'Johnny' continued to plead frantically for his friends help, especially in light of the fact that he ('Johnny') was loaned clothing, and was invited to join them on their usual roaming expedition that turned sour. In response to 'Johnny's plea for help, another of the AJ dad's friends used his sling to shoot 'Harry' in his lower back; causing 'Harry' to simultaneously release 'Johnny' while clutching to his back with a grimace on his face. 'Johnny', the AJ's dad and his other friends ran away from the scene, pledging never to return there again. Lessons learnt!

Another of the AJ dad's storytelling exploits surrounded another of his many pronouncements; for example, avoid calling persons derogatory names. In this case, the AJ's father told him of another of his many stories which involved his childhood friends. He recalled an incident when he and his childhood friends played a prank on another (new) acquaintance; who eventually became friends to them all. The story began like this:

According to the AJ' dad, he said that there was a man in his community who was given a derogatory name called 'Monkey Enus'. Soon thereafter, a new three member family moved into the AJ dad's neighborhood; comprising of a child called 'Gregory' and his parents. The man called 'Monkey Enus' was known to everybody in the community except for the new guy.

In a bid to show this new child around the community, the AJ's father said that he and his childhood friends took 'Gregory' for a walk around the neighborhood. During the first fateful stroll of walking together on the road, one of the AJ dad's childhood friends encouraged 'Gregory' to shout the names 'Monkey Enus' aloud. He complied.

'Gregory' was asked to do so again by calling out the names 'Monkey Enus' again, while passing a man along the way. The child complied again to the AJ's dad friends' wishes. According to the AJ dad's story, he and his friends knew that the approaching man was called that nickname 'Monkey Enus' and he (the said man) hated being called same.

However, this information about the man was not told to the new guy 'Gregory', who by this time was enjoying bellowing the names aloud. The new guy was walloped in his face by the approaching man- the impact sent 'Gregory' sprawling backwards across the pavement. The AJ's dad and his childhood friends ran away from the scene laughing at the new guy 'Gregory'. Lessons learnt!

In short, the AJ recalled that he had fun living with his dad. Of interest, the AJ said that his father enjoyed the experience of seeing at least two of his sons completing university level education, pursued successful careers. However, he was not alive to either witness the AJ's first marriage ceremony or the birth of his daughter. Well, that is life is it not?

## The Legacy of the AJ – pioneering activities

As early as ten years old, the AJ wondered what type of contribution to humanity would he make, and how may he be able to do so. The AJ wondered with much intrigue how would that be possible, and will he ever be given or allowed the opportunity to effectively make his mark on the 'world map' of life; especially by the 'movers and shakers' of the world.

How weird could it get for the AJ? Imagine a child of his age (then); (a) witnessing the challenges of being a part of the AJ's parents' dysfunctional family, (b) getting ready to do examinations for entry into secondary school (with limited resources, help and advice from his elders), and knowing that the availability of role models were deemed 'scare commodities'. Despite his reality, the AJ recalled seizing the few opportunities available to him at that time to begin honing his skills; especially through his involvement in church activities and scouting.

One may ask, at age 10, what skills could the AJ be honing, that may cause the world, his country, his community and his family to remember him by? Should the AJ be focusing on living and enjoying life instead of considering how others will recount his contribution to the World?

Perhaps, it could be argued that anyone who attempted to think thoughts like those of the AJ -at such an early age- may be found to adopt same only if (a) one had been afflicted with a terminal disease that allowed one to live for less than five more years on earth, or (b) one had bouts of lunacy. Fortunately, for the AJ, he was neither terminally ill nor mad.

The childhood reflections of the AJ revealed that he had some unique skills that caused him to be targeted, admired, misunderstood, and chastised by most persons that he interacted with. The AJ noticed that he was an 'alternative thinker', a good manager/ organizer and had an infectious personality. By being an 'alternative thinker', this trait attracted both admirers and skeptics. Many of the persons who asked the AJ for his opinion on any subject/ topical issue were not only startled by his comments (as many of them often retorted that they did not interpret (look at) it that way before), but the others were revolted by them.

The AJ's voice changed when he was about eleven years old, and he was in first form at high school. Coincidentally, the AJ was three feet nine inches tall at the time, when he became equipped with a base voice. This voice change activity had unexpectedly thrown the AJ into the full view of the Public. The AJ discovered that persons were only focusing on listening to the sound of his voice, and not on the contents of his speech; which eventually became annoying to him. Of interest, many of the AJ's friends took pleasure in interfering with him; in order to get the AJ to say something to them.

Between the ages of eleven and seventeen years old, the AJ was able to hone his skills as an organizer, when he was elected to, and/or appointed to many positions of leadership in the various clubs/organizations at school, church or in the community. Having being given those opportunities to lead from 'in front', the AJ was able to pioneering things. Ooh, yes, whatever tasks that the AJ embarked on, he was able to 'break new grounds of achievements' and superseded all expectations.

Despite the complexities of life mentioned earlier (such as obtaining limited counseling and guidance from his elders, coupled with diminishing numbers of role models being made available to emulate) the AJ wanted to be a policymaker. These thoughts began to take shape in his mind while in upper sixth form at high school. He wondered how to go about becoming a policymaker, and what impact achieving this career choice might have on the legacy of the AJ. At what level of policy should the AJ attempt to influence? At this point, the AJ decided on how he could be an effective policymaker in this life!

Interestingly, it was on becoming an adult that the AJ got the opportunities to engage in pertinent activities; which ultimately allowed him to effect positive changes at the community level in his country. For example, as a consequence of the AJ's unconventional thoughts (which originated from being an 'alternative thinker'), he discovered that many persons and interest groups wanted to hear his opinion on various topical issues. Of note, while the pattern of thought of the AJ may attract many, it also caused him to be hated by some; especially the persons who were in higher (perceived) status position than the AJ.

The AJ could easily recall/ mention numerous occasions when his expressed thoughts have cause him to be deprived of opportunities to advance in his working and educational environment; despite knowing that the display of his skills will benefit the organization. He also knew of occasions when his ideas were not only 'shot down' by those persons in hierarchical positions of committees (at work and/or in various community based organizations) but they were adopted and used by these same persons at a later date; without due consideration as to where the source of their information originated from. Interesting is it not?

With respect to the AJ's pioneering activities, many stories came to mind. As early as age 17, the AJ –as a member of at least one of his church youth groups- worked on several projects that surpassed all fundraising and new membership 'drive' targets.

The life of the AJ took on an additional dimension when he became a member of the workforce (for the first and only time) at approximately twenty years old. For your information, the AJ tried to get a summer job on at least three occasions; prior to doing major examinations; the General Certificate of Education at the Ordinary Level (GCE 'O' Level). However, the prospective employers said that he was overqualified for the positions being applied for in their organizations. Strange situations don't you think?

Anyway, since his employment, the AJ have been able to, and enjoyed doing many activities of which, often lead to possibly enhancing his legacy. For example, as early as approximately six months after being employed, the AJ had to tackle a specific problem presented to him by his supervisor. Having thought about the situation, the AJ formulated a solution and presented it to his supervisor. The supervisor not only vigorously disagreed with the solution presented to her by the AJ, but she insisted that her (other) solution be applied to solve the problem that the AJ was presented with. The AJ's objected to her proposal; an action that lead her to complain to the chief project manager.

Two investigations were launched into the alleged unprofessional behavior of the AJ towards his supervisor of which: (a) the first outcome lead to the AJ receiving a warning letter from the chief project manager, and the job was reassigned to another officer, and; (b) the second outcome lead to the AJ being exonerated from all charges.

Of interest - about six weeks months later - it was discovered that the solution that the AJ had originally proposed to solve that unique problem mentioned earlier, was adopted and used to solve all problems of that specific nature, throughout the life of the project. The AJ did not receive any acknowledgment for the devising the solution from the hierarchy of command.

The AJ used the opportunity to remind the said supervisor of the impact of her reluctance to implement his solution to the problem (already identified earlier in this chapter) on the efficiency of the project. Coincidentally, approximately six months later, the AJ was the only individual selected from his office to attend a study program; administered by one of the local universities. Shortly after completing this course, the AJ was transferred to work in another division of the organization, located elsewhere in the country.

Having being employed for approximately three years, the AJ became a paying member of his office's sports and social club. In a few years later, the AJ was elected to several top positions of the club-ranging from the Sports Coordinator to the President. During his tenure as President of the said club, the AJ not only implemented a major fundraising activity that allowed the club to earn income for posterity, but he also provided an outlet for its staff members to enter the annual national cultural and culinary festival competitions. Interestingly, some of the top participants of the office culinary and art competitions have also won medals at the national level.

Over the years of employment, the AJ have pioneered the development and implementation of at least two work related processes-using the 'visionary approach' available to him- prior to the full office technical integration of these processes. In fact, these processes were immediately adopted for widespread use in the office, because of the overall benefits that have accrued from their collective implementations (such as the enhanced accessibility, portability, storage and retrieval opportunities at the office).

Looking at the AJ's legacy from the societal perspective, he has written several letters that were published in the print media on social, political and sporting issues. In fact, most of these letters have not only helped to re-shape the landscape of his country, but they also helped to instill civic pride in his fellow-nationals.

The AJ was fortunate and delighted to be a member of a few social organizations in his country. Indeed, he enjoyed the pleasure of working (with his fellow nationals and foreigners) to develop and implement programs that were mutually beneficial to all, while enhancing international goodwill in the world.

In 1999, for example, the AJ benefited from receiving a six - month training course in Asia. On his return home, the AJ became an alumni member of the sponsoring agency that funded the training program that he attended.

Three years later, he was elected to the top position of that group. During his tenure at President of the organization, the AJ worked with: (a) his fellow alumni members; (b) other organizations sharing similar intrinsic values as the alumni group, and; (c) foreign nationals originating from the host Asian country that facilitated his study, to stage an extraordinary cross – national cultural experience of unprecedented proportions, ever held in his country.

Of interest, while studying in this Asian country mentioned earlier, the AJ and his fellow countryman were part of a touring party that attended a peace rally; being held in one of the largest parks of this nation's capital city. They were introduced to the top executive of this international peace advocacy group- the host of the said peace rally. At this point of his recollection, the AJ could not anticipate how weird this experience could get for him, until he felt the impact of that experience on his life, a few months later.

Could you imagine that the female executive member of the international peace advocacy group that met the AJ and his fellow countryman at the said peace rally (for less than two minutes) came to visit them in his country for a week, and accompanied by five of her fellow countrywomen? Also, these ladies came to his country - fully equipped - to perform the same peace ceremony rituals that were witnessed in their homeland. According to the AJ, all of them performed three of the four peace rituals together at different locations, across his homeland.

The AJ was given the option to choose the fourth site for performing the final peace ceremony ritual.

Well, after a few months delay, the AJ's choice of venue for the conduct of the fourth (and final) peace ceremony ritual in his country landed him in guiding! How weird could this get for the AJ? Ooh yes, the AJ became one of the few men who ever headed one of the umbrella organizations responsible for overseeing the operations of Girl Guides movement in his country!

Please note that the drama continued for the AJ. On one of the many occasions, the AJ was among many persons who were invited to attend a birthday party, which was held in honor of the Head of State of the said Asian country that he studied for six months in 1999 (and hosted by the embassy of the said Asian country). Early in the function, the AJ's national Head of State addressed this esteemed audience. The AJ overheard his nation's Head of State making reference to the impact of the activities that were done by the AJ and his friends at one of the four venues that the peace ceremony rituals were held on the promotion of international goodwill and greater collaboration between both nations. For example, the Head of State mentioned that tourists were visiting the site; as a testimony of his nation's participation in the preservation of world peace initiatives.

At the end of the function, the national Head of State found out that the AJ – one of the principal persons responsible for creating that landmark situation – was also in attendance. He (the Head of State) not only shook and held unto the hand of the AJ (for approximately fifteen minutes while greeting the fellow audience members who wished to acknowledge his presence at the function), but he engaged him in an impromptu, exclusive and private conversation. The AJ mentioned that they shared fond memories of their working and interpersonal experiences with the foreign nationals of the Asian country that hosted the birthday function.

On a different note, over the years, the AJ has observed this scenario mentioned below. Whenever the AJ has been a part of an audience or any group, as soon as he spoke and/or to make a contribution to the proceedings, he often became drafted into select groups; so that his work can be utilized to the benefit of all.

The AJ stated that his latest episode at being apart of doing pioneering activities occurred a few months ago, after attending an internationally sponsored meeting. As a result of making a contribution to the proceedings of this meeting, another member of the same meeting invited the AJ to make another presentation to this national body (which was in its embryonic stage of development) a few days later. How weird could this get? As soon as The AJ complied with this person's wishes, the AJ was immediately included on the executive body of this national organization as an ex-officio member. Simultaneously, the AJ was required to, and has already started to represent this national body at various functions at the highest level, among other things. In a few months, the AJ was endorsed in the position on the executive body of the said national organization, at its annual conference.

Given the information being disclosed to all, on reflection of the life of the AJ to date, some of the persons may have concluded that reasons why persons would want to remember the AJ could be forwarded. In addition, some of these people have already thought that the AJ has started to generate a legacy worth noting. What do you say?

## What makes the AJ different from everyone else?

Over the years, it has been argued in many circles, as to what caused the AJ to be different from everyone else. Of course, the obvious things such as the uniqueness surrounding his birthing circumstances, and the inherited physical distinguishing features should not be a point for consideration, ok? With those matters out the way, then, perhaps, the focus of this difference should be on how the hidden traits that helped the AJ to shape his personality, character and integrity.

In his opinion, the AJ thought that it was the combined impact of the use of the traits that shaped his personality, character and integrity; causing him to be further separated from his fellow human beings. If you still have doubts about this claim, let us investigate it further, ok?

What was so unique about his personality that allowed the AJ to be different than others? AJ noticed that his diction, the choice of words that his used in conversation with people, and his body language have caused many persons to take serious note of him. The AJ was aware of the observation mentioned earlier from as early as when he was approximately 11 years old. Soon thereafter, when his voice changed at twelve years of age, the addition of that feature plus his diminutive stature to the abovementioned only intensified the attention given to AJ by other persons.

The AJ often asked himself the following questions: How weird could it get? Could someone possess a unique combination of traits such as being:
- Jovial yet serious;
- Placid yet emotive;
- 'Steel willed' yet compassionate;
- An observant and be discrete;
- Firm (disciplinarian) yet flexible;
- Ruthless and yet thoughtful when making decisions;
- Loving and/or harsh with respect to making decisions concerning personal emotions;
- Dynamic yet reserved, and;
- Articulate yet conservative?

Most people who have interacted with the AJ over the years, have mentioned to him and others that he possessed all of the personality attributes described above, plus more.

Could someone possess such a complex set of personality traits mentioned earlier (as that of the AJ) and be similar to everybody else in the world?

Of interest, because the AJ had to deal with the fact that he has complex personality traits, several persons who have to interact with him have sometimes expressed that they either misunderstood him or his intentions or both. In that light, the AJ has already accepted that his disposition often constituted an 'occupational hazard' when he interacted with others. As a result; he has not been deterred by the outcomes of in his deliberations with other persons, ever...

On a different note, the AJ used the benefits of the adoption of certain attitudes to life and its experiences, as well as and his inherently complex personality traits in such a way that they all contributed to the formation of his unique character. Ooh yes. What could constitute the features of this so-called 'unique' character that the AJ possessed?

According to the AJ, the features of the his character comprised of being; (a) meticulous, (b) contrite, (c) trustworthy, (d) confidential, (e) bold, (f) very thoughtful of others, (g) secretive, (h) genuine, (i) courteous, (j) forceful yet tender, (k) dependable and (l) reliable. Again the typical question can be asked in this presentation. Can anyone possess such a combination of character features (as that of the AJ) yet, not 'deemed' different from everybody else in the world?

If you have not been convinced that the information revealed so far to you showed that AJ has to be different from other human beings 'on the face of the earth', more evidence shall be forthcoming. If the AJ has been endowed with both (a) a complex personality and (b) multiple featured attributes depicting the strength of his character, then this individual ought to show that he possessed integrity. This has been the 'cry' of the majority of people who stated; that the AJ portrayed the characteristics of an individual of integrity!

Interestingly, these statements did not originate from the AJ. The collection of statements and the analogies inferred from them were made by many persons who had reason to interact with the AJ, over time. For example, it has been said that the AJ has revealed that his behavior has been guided by the tenets of integrity in his deliberations with all persons. These persons often stated that the AJ displayed acts of incorruptibility, honesty and fortitude in all of his dealings with everyone; despite their age, social status, religious persuasions, and endowments in life.

Finally, given all the information disclosed earlier, can it be said that the AJ has not shown that he possessed the uniqueness that caused him to be viewed as a different human being when compared to the others? You have no choice but to respond by saying yes.

## The AJ - the source of controversy

It has been noted that some people's reaction to the AJ's contribution to life issues, conversation, and his behavior (such as being self-sufficient) often result in bouts of controversy. Often, the AJ not only wondered how weird could these situations get for him, but also about the implications thereof. In fact, sometimes, the situations got weirder that anticipated. There have been times when the controversial conditions have not been confined to the frequency of its occurrences, but these conditions have broaden its reach and scope in such a way that tend to affect every area of life of the AJ.

Over the years, the thoughts of being viewed as the source of controversy used to bother the AJ. This was so, especially when all he wanted to do was to make his contribution, to be benefit of both the society and the world at large, without offending anyone.

However, after some deep periodic self-analysis, the AJ discovered the following: (a) he not only found out why persons viewed his contributions to the wider society in controversial terms, but; (b) he also became comfortable with himself, his special endowments, and his abilities to make decisions that can withstand public scrutiny.

In addition, the AJ knew that, and have already accepted the fact that he has a special type and quality of endowments that he was privileged to possess such as:
- The complex personality traits;
- The interesting mix of character features that guide how the AJ viewed life, and its issues;
- The 'professed' integrity;
- Being an alternative thinker;
- Certain patterns of behavior such as being self-sufficient and confident.

Coupled with the discoveries itemized earlier, the AJ also appreciated the reality that he would be, and has been adjudged based on his previous activities, achievements, and contributions to the society.

In that light, when all things mentioned earlier were considered, it would not be difficult for one to conceive the notion that many persons who (viewed the actions of the AJ in controversial ways and,) had reason to interact with the AJ, to express their reluctance in support of any suggestions made by him on matters under discussion.

Despite having the unique endowments, the AJ has accepted the reality that these persons who viewed him as the source of controversy either react unfavorably to his opinions/suggestions forwarded on the matter, or be stimulated to present contesting views on matters being discussed. The reactions of these persons usually occurred after hearing/ or being exposure to the principles that dictate how the AJ viewed life and its issues, or his opinion/suggestion forwarded on the matter under scrutiny.

The AJ had already adopted certain principles that helped to shape his character as early as in his childhood years. For example, He habitually sought after, and spoke the truth at all times. The AJ usually strived to tackle and correctly/accurately complete any task that he undertook, on his first attempt. However, many persons do not usually and consistently practice the abovementioned approaches, as the AJ did. Whenever these persons have to do activities that would cause them to interact with the AJ, controversial outcomes (such as verbal disagreements, quarrels, and behavior problems) usually resulted.

Whenever a resolution to the problem has been found, the AJ has been amazed to discover a 'typically' surprising development, worth noting. When calm has been restored between/among the conflicting parties, these persons/ groups usually adopt the suggestions forwarded by the AJ. In these circumstances, the AJ had reasons to wonder why there was a disagreement on the topic in the first place, especially when the initial suggestion made by him was eventually used. How weird could that revelation be to the AJ?

At this point, let us deal with some of the many circumstances that demonstrated how the life of the AJ impacted these persons in such a way that it generated controversial outcomes. Let us begin with the home and neighborhood front.

At home, for obvious reasons, the AJ has elected not to dispose of his garbage by burning. That is, he properly placed his garbage in garbage bags, and allowed the municipal city disposal trucks to collect them. However, some of his neighbors have chosen to dispose of their garbage by burning; to the detriment to the environment, and the creation of personal health problems. The AJ have had many confrontations with these individuals over this matter, to the extent that some of these persons have elected to malice him.

Interestingly, there was an occasion when one of the AJ's neighbors attempted to dispose of their garbage by burning, on a day when the AJ went to work. This action (of burning the garbage) not only caused the fire to rage out of control, but the fire also burnt the public utility electric wire leading to the house of the AJ. This fire deprived the AJ of electricity for at least one day. This neighbor immediately fled the scene (and the area) before the AJ arrived home from work that fateful night.

Ooh, the AJ had to institute several measures to protect his property from everybody - even the state utility companies. How weird was that?

The property/home of the AJ possessed a manicured lawn, a lovely arranged garden of flowers, many Ackee and Mango fruit trees, as well as Banana trees, and it has a swing made to seat two persons.

The interesting thing about this house was that it was; (a) located near a primary school, (b) in a neighborhood that mainly comprised of students and employed persons, and (c) plagued with pradial thieves (with some of them being drug addicts) and wild animals that were allowed to invade and feed on other people's properties without their permission. In addition, some of the neighbors aided and abetted the pradial thieves by purchasing some of their exploits from them, such as the stolen fruits, and there were some public utility company workers who often ignore proper practices when entering and/or leaving ones private properties when conducting legitimate business on these properties.

Given the above mentioned sets of scenarios, often, the AJ had to take decisive action to prevent the property from all the persons and animals involved in defiling the sanctity of the premises.

First, on numerous occasions, the AJ had to physically challenge and overpower the pradial thieves who stole fruits from the premises. To date, his premises have been spared of the menace, the onslaught and plunder that usually occurred after the pradial thieves visited. In fact, the AJ was not only able to restore his privacy on the compound, but he was able to reap and share his produce with whomever he wished; without being in competition with the pradial thieves, to get the produce. Of interest, the same pradial thieves have also given the AJ some respectful names such as Elder, and Justice; reflecting their acknowledgment of his sole right to exercise his preferences on his premises.

Second, in order to protect his investment, the AJ had to curtail entry of the utility workers to the property, because to their bad habits when they collectively entered and left his premises; in pursuit of their legitimate business on the compound. Why? The pradial thieves and other unwanted persons took note of the behavior of the utility workers who visited the premises. After completing their legitimate business on the compound the utility workers usually left the gate opened. This unthinking action allowed the thieves, and stray animals free entry to plunder the premises. Eventually, these entities were forced to change their behavior towards the AJ. How weird could that get for the AJ?

Third, as a result of the unthinking actions of the utility workers, causing stray animals to enter the premises and feed on the flowers, the AJ had to spend more money to heighten the perimeter fencing around of the compound. Phew, the elevation of the fencing not only kept out the stray animals, but it also prevented unwanted/uninvited guests from using the home of the AJ as an amusement park. (Remember, the AJ has a swing that seated two persons, in his yard.)

Interesting, some of the confrontations that the AJ had with a few of his neighbors surrounded how they wanted to use his property; which was contrary to his principles. For example, some of these neighbors wanted to get access to the first crops from off the premises, yet they were not prepared to clean up the leaves from the trees when they (the leaves) fell on their side of the fence. How weird could that get? Has the AJ ever complied with their wishes? Of course not! In fact, the AJ's objection to their behavior caused the entire family of this household to malice him, and moved away to live elsewhere.

If you thought that example was weird, check this out. The time came for the AJ to upgrade his mode of transport, after driving the older car for approximately ten years. Having bought a new car, the AJ decided to sell the older one.

After some consideration, the AJ chose the individual who he wanted to sell the car to. This individual was not the highest bidder, but he was a long standing family friend and utility guy for at least three of my immediate neighbors.

The AJ and this individual agreed to the terms in which the car shall be sold. On discovery that the car was up for sale, at least one of the AJ's neighbors tried to inveigle him into selling the vehicle to them, instead of to the individual to whom the contractual agreement was already enforced. At every attempt, the AJ had graciously declined their monetary enticements in favor of his original buyer; as the AJ maintained his principled position on the matter.

Immediately after the car was sold to the original buyer, the neighbors who were interested in, and made many efforts to persuade the AJ to sell them the car, did something extremely weird. They not only simultaneously withdrew their friendship from the fellow who bought the car from the AJ, but they collectively prevented him from earning any further income from them, and anyone that they knew who could provide this individual with 'potential' jobs.

It was amazing that these neighbors penalized this man because the AJ could not be swayed from off his principles; pertaining to his decision on who to sell his car to. Remember, this man was their handyman and family friend for many years! Wow, how weird did this get for the AJ?

On a different note, how did the confrontations situations occur between the AJ and others in the working environment? Remember that the AJ still maintained the main features of his character; which tended to separate him from others. Given this reality, it did not make interactions between the AJ and persons (or groups of persons) in the office environment any easier than which obtained in his home environment.

The first confrontation situation that occurred between the AJ and another person – his supervisor- took place approximately six months after he was employed. A problem occurred with the task being assigned to the AJ; which was taken to his supervisor for her help and advice. She posited an approach to solving the problem, which in his opinion, was inadequate to effectively tackle the problem at hand. She reacted badly to the suggestion that the AJ made, escalated the situation to the extent that he was reported to their manager of the project.

Two investigations were launched into the matter, which ultimately lead to him being exonerated from all charges, and the task was reassigned to someone else.

Approximately six weeks later, the identical task that caused the controversy was returned to the AJ; using his suggestion that he forwarded to solving the problem. In fact, his original suggestion forwarded at the time of the controversy was not only adopted, but it was used to solve any other problem of that type by the office. Interesting was it not?

The AJ has - by virtue of his wealth of experiences, alternative thinking attributes, among other things – been invited to attend many meetings and be placed on several committees. Often, the expressed suggestions of the AJ have not only been heatedly contested by individuals and groups of individuals in attendance to the committee meetings, but, on many occasions, these individuals eventually agreed with them. How weird could this get?

The AJ often wondered what could be the motivation behind these persons who initially chose to oppose his suggestions/ contributions presented to the committee meetings, only to agree with them in the end. Of interest, majority of persons who interacted with the AJ in any meeting setting do not anticipate that he would be a non-participant in these meetings (even by being quiet), as the groups expect to receive his contribution to the proceedings.

Despite the controversial moments that may have occurred at the office, the average person appreciated the contributions made by the AJ, in any forum that people gather to discuss issues of importance. In addition, as a result of their 'perceived leadership potential' of the AJ, many of these persons also elected him represent them in any forum of that nature.

Based on the reaction of people, the AJ was forced to grapple with some thoughts that flowed in his mind. For example, how could a man 'deemed as being controversial' attract the high quality type of honor and respect of his co-workers across all hierarchical boundaries? In addition, how could such a controversial person properly represent them on vital committees- integral to the general staff welfare at his office?

Of interest, the identical general outcomes surrounding the AJ's interactions with persons at his office also obtained, when he communicated with others in both the social and personal arenas.

However, it had be noted that whenever the AJ spoke to people - especially in a personal/ intimate setting – the first reactions of these recipients to the statement(s)) uttered to them usually seemed to cause them to immediately erect a 'defensive language barrier' between them and him. In these circumstances, the AJ also noticed that the said persons who were spoken to initially, shortly after repeating whatever he said in his original statement to them, (without changing a word in the original sentence,) suddenly drop their 'barriers' and indicated that they understood what was originally intended to be communicated to them. AJ often wondered what could cause these persons to initially react to his speech in that manner, only to change their behavior soon thereafter.

If you thought that that those questions mentioned earlier were weird, then consider this outcome. Often, there have been occasions, whereby several of the women who; while they were intimately linked to the AJ at the time, objected to an approach forwarded to them by him. Soon after the love relationship ended, these said women readily adopted the suggestions/approaches that were originally mentioned by the AJ, to solve the problem that existed during the relationship.

How weird could that get for the AJ? Why object to an idea presented to you initially, only to adopt it (without any alterations) in the end? Yikes, such has been the live experiences of the AJ.

In summary, the AJ understood that life and living without moments of controversy ought to be boring, indeed. Hence, instead of retreating into obscurity, the AJ embraced whatever life had to offer him.

## Dealing with love and its challenges-as a teenager

Wow, what a topic to deal with – love and its challenges! The love life of the AJ has been very interesting indeed. He began experiencing love and its challenges from as early as when he was 13 years old. (As mentioned before, at that age, the AJ was three feet nine inches tall, with a bass voice, 'kind of cute' looking' and possessed a dynamic personality.) At this age, the AJ not only had a hard time managing the pressures of the opposite sex, but he also had to keep their many advances a secret (and private) from everyone else. Why? It was because the actions of the ladies - note not the girls - were very explicit, and for all to see.

Remember, the AJ began experiencing the kinds of pressures from the ladies; of course which was good for his ego, at age 13. As of that time, everyday when the AJ went to school; he had at least one weird event that happened with the AJ and a woman/girl.

During those instances, the AJ experienced women (a) groping him, (b) rubbing him down, (c) caressing him without his permission, (d) whining on him both in front of and behind him, (e) kissing him, (f) receiving love notes, (g) providing him with invitations to attend private intimate parties, (h) and invading him when he was using the bathrooms. In addition, these women provided AJ with invitations to touch (grope) them, did death defying acts in order to get his attention, introduced him to other women/ girls, and they seduced him. There were occasions when the AJ had to wash his uniform before he arrived home from school in the evenings; because his shirt got smudged with lipstick stains and/or the scent of women's perfume.

Of interest, the AJ was also a sportsman at school, and of course, it (being a sportsman) had its own sets of 'female love challenges' to be tackled, on a daily basis.

As the AJ grew older (and taller), the female love pressures being brought to bear on him only intensified. It became so pressurizing on the AJ that, at one point, his father had to intervene on his behalf; in order to ensure that (in his opinion,) his son would be able to 'live long enough' to become a man. On a few occasions, the AJ's Dad had to remind some of the women who were visibly pressuring his son sexually, that he was not an adult male as yet. In addition, the AJ's Dad tried to encourage these women to seek companionship with men of their own age range, instead of 'robbing the cradle.'

On the first occasion that the AJ heard his father complaining about his son's love predicament, he laughed. However, later in life, the AJ understood the wisdom in his father's argument. The implications of the arguments were significant for the AJ, especially when he had to learn how to effectively handle these love challenges (plus completing his studies and household chores, interact with family, attend church services and other civic functions); while preparing to be a responsible productive human being in society.

As a man, many of the things mentioned earlier, occurred to the AJ, but many of his love life experiences with the opposite sex were not only weird, but were astonishing in nature.

Before going any further, the AJ wanted to disclose a few of his thoughts to you the reader. For example, he thought that the success of love interactions between heterosexual couples were often predicated on a number of factors, namely; (a) the socialization and upbringing of both parties, (b) the attitude and willingness of both parties to work at, and building/maintaining a healthy relationship and (c) ones skills set of other endowments that one possessed which one has decided to share with each other in such a relationship. In addition, the AJ thought that, depending on how each factor mentioned above interplayed on the objectives in the relationship, coupled with the impact of the influences of the family networks on the love relationships of the couple; the outcome, type and durability of the love relationship may become either strong or fragile.

Well, the AJ had experienced almost every type and form of heterosexual love relationships ever encountered as a human being on earth.., or that was what he claimed. Anyway, enough for the lyrics and platitudes! At this point, the AJ shall seek to illustrate a few of the many events that happened to him; to explain in brief, some of the love challenges that the he had to deal with in his life so far.

The AJ recalled attending church (when he was about 13 years old), with his mother and siblings. At about an hour and a half into the service, on that fateful Sunday morning, he received a note from a female in the congregation requesting his audience with her in the vestry. He not only thought of using the opportunity to comply with the wishes of the lady, but he could also use the bathroom. As soon as the AJ entered the vestry – en route - to the bathroom, he felt someone grabbing him from behind (as if he was being abducted). In a continuous motion, this individual (happily, for the AJ, the person was a woman) instantly spun him around, and gave him a lush, passionate kiss.

Can you imagine how surprised the AJ was, when he was officially introduced to this woman for the first time, after being nabbed and passionately kissed by this woman? Wow, the saga continued. At that said church, the AJ could almost predict that he would encounter the similar situation mentioned earlier, every third Sunday of the month for four months consecutively; with a different girl/woman. The AJ left that church; never to return, after the fifth month of that ordeal!

How weird could that get for the AJ? In fact, it got weirder for him, as the girls were there in abundance for him. The situations became so challenging for the AJ to handle, that on many occasions, some of his friends benefited from some of his exploits with the females.

There were occasions when the AJ overheard parents of some of the girls doing prospecting of him; on behalf of their daughters! In some cases the parents used the AJ as their 'testing ground' before allowing their daughters, nieces, or younger sisters to get a chance at being intimate with him. According to the AJ, all these activities mentioned earlier happened to him when he was a teenager. Wow, can you imagine that? In addition, the AJ said he had to conceal these strange situations from his mother and siblings; primarily because some of his mother's friends were guilty of these sexual overplays and advances being experienced by him too!

Although the heterosexual relationship pressures were intense, the AJ admitted (or confessed) that he did not understand either the intricacies of love or what The AJ and his friend coordinated a church beach outing; an event that was very successful indeed. As customary - at the end of the day- after a full day of swimming, fun and frolic, everybody was instructed tit entailed; especially from a woman's perspective, until he was older.

At 14 years old, the AJ remembered interacting with a good looking, fat but well contoured girl (who possessed a wonderful personality), for a limited time at church. He met her in the church hallway by accident, while having a conversation with one of his friends. Apparently, she seemed to be intrigued with the conversation that was being held, came over towards the AJ, held his hands and began massaging them. The friend who was conversing with the AJ noticed what was happening to him, abruptly ended the conversation, and left him to the whims of this girl. Both of them spoke to each other briefly (as that was the only thing that the AJ could do at the time-while being overwhelmed both by her beauty and advances), then parted company to return home to their respective families.

A few weeks later, the AJ saw this young lady in the company of an older friend of his – in a relatively lonely spot – while attending to him in a 'gentle manner'. The following day, at church, she wanted to have a conversation with the AJ; an offer he gently declined. This young lady was not only visibly upset with the decision, but she asked the AJ what was the problem on many occasions; to no avail. After lodging another of her many appeals to the AJ, she visited his home and tried to get his mother to assist her at obtaining an answer to her question. That method did not work, and she went away feeling dejected. Shortly afterwards, she did not return to that place of worship again.

It was later in life that the AJ eventually understood the issue he had to learn how to deal with; the typical issue surrounding human jealousy. Being adults, (happily for the AJ,) he learnt that the said young lady still loved him; despite his crude behavior then.

The AJ noted that there were at least four occasions when- contrary to the experiences of many men- he was 'swamped' by women, (some of whom the AJ were neither aware of, nor acquainted with before the 'swamping encounters',) at the point when he was actually having sex with the woman that he was intimately involved with. Ooh, these occasions have not only been weird for the AJ, but he has had difficulty forgetting them!

Could you consider this scenario for a minute? Perhaps, it would be considered a nice feeling for the men who were intentionally or reluctantly invited to participate in the sex act with a woman in the same sexual session; even if these men forced themselves on her. However, can you imagine if two or more women were intentionally or reluctantly invited to have sex with the same man in the same sexual session; even if these women forced themselves unto him? Well, these activities happened to the AJ. In fact, he was pounced upon by more than one woman simultaneously demanding to be 'serviced', while he was actually having sex with another woman; twice at a party, once on the beach, and once while tutoring one of his mother's friend in her home. Of note, these activities occurred to the AJ before he was 20 years old.

The AJ remembered meeting one of his 'eventual' girlfriends on the beach; at a beach outing that his friend and he coordinated on behalf of one of the church groups that they were executive officers of. How did this happen? o get ready to leave the venue by a specified time.

To comply with the general instructions issued earlier, the AJ went to the changing room to change his clothes; from his swim trunks to his ordinary clothes. While the AJ was in the act of changing his clothing, that is, removing his swim trunks to put on his underpants, a young lady- who attended the same beach outing-barged into the male changing room and caught him 'with his pants down'. To his amazement, the young lady looked at the AJ's naked body, smiled and then left the room.

A few weeks later, this said young lady (who barged into the changing room while the AJ was changing his clothes) and he became intimate friends; a relationship that lasted 2 years, until she migrated to another country.

The AJ remembered another occasion that caused him to meet a young lady - whom he became intimate with for at least 2 years -before she also migrated to another country. In this case, the AJ was walking towards a group of girls who were conversing with each other. On passing this group, the AJ overheard one of the girls saying to them that she hated him. Upon hearing the comment, the AJ retraced his steps, went over towards the young lady who spoke those words, and whispered in her ears saying "Were you so sure that your comment was true?" Afterwards, the AJ smiled and continued his original journey.

Coincidentally, this young lady knew the AJ's brothers and their home address. Given the fact that she and her female relative usually visited the AJ's home on a regular basis, the AJ ensured that he was conveniently absent from his home, whenever she opted to visit. The activity of making himself absent from his home whenever this young lady chose to visit went on for approximately six months.

One day in the seventh month of being conveniently scare, the AJ eventually had to pass this young lady's house. On passing her house, he was surprised when she ran outside the house towards him, and displayed an uncharacteristic impulsive, spontaneous and loud greeting, coupled with a powerful embrace- all of which took place in the street. She also reprimanded the AJ by telling him never to do that (of avoiding her) again, ever. She immediately confessed to the AJ that he was correct about her emotional feelings for him; in that, she did not hate him, but it was the opposite of that.

Shortly afterwards, both of them entered into an intimate relationship with each other, lasting for approximately 2 years. Of interest, an unfortunate event occurred- causing the demise of this relationship. Soon thereafter, this young lady migrated to another country. How weird could that get for the AJ?

Another of the AJ's girlfriends had to migrate while they were intimately involved with each other. Coincidentally, most of his early relationships ended prematurely when these ladies migrated to live abroad.

There have been occasions when a misunderstanding may cause interpersonal interactions to become challenging to deal with. For example, a female friend (fictionally called 'Jackie') whose mother moved her away from the area - and from the AJ- before any intimacy could be considered.

Interestingly, 'Jackie' - five years his junior- lived in a two family household comprising of six persons.

It was noted that 'Jackie' was having difficulty understanding how to interpret the information that her teacher taught her in school. Therefore, the AJ was asked to help 'Jackie' with her homework; a job he was good at. Apparently, one of 'Jackie's' mother's female friends was uncomfortable with the assistance given to 'Jackie'; although the instructions were being re-taught in the public domain, and in full view of the parents of the other family. This woman complained to 'Jackie's' mother about something, and as a result, 'Jackie' and her mother not only immediately moved away from the house, but they moved out of my life, until 25 years later.

Ooh yes, it was 25 years later that 'Jackie' met the AJ and told him several things that occurred to her back then. For example, she told the AJ of; (a) the complaint that her mother's friend made to her mother, and (b) the severe beating that she received from her mother on that fateful night, as a result of the complaint.

'Jackie said that she tried unsuccessfully to explain that the allegation made of her by the mother's friend was false; implying that the AJ was positioning himself to become intimate with her. 'Jackie' told the AJ that she was not able to convince her mother that the AJ was professional in his activities, and the relationship with both of them was platonic. 'Jackie's mother- being enraged by the complaint- not only punished her, but immediately moved the family away from the neighborhood, without any prior notice whatsoever!

Interestingly, 'Jackie' eventually told the AJ that she had loved him over 25 years ago, and despite the obvious reality, she still loved him. Shortly after a few subsequent meetings, she asked the AJ to make love to her; a request he complied with. It was noted that this relationship could not be sustainable, because of the interpersonal relationship 'gap' which was caused by the 25 year separation and lifestyle changes that resulted.

As a teenager, the AJ continued to experience many more situations (some of them being classified as 'weird' events). Of course, several of these events have to be treated as 'classified' and cannot be disclosed under any circumstances whatsoever. Despite these realities, all pertinent lessons have been learnt.

In that light, the teenager AJ -having being exposed to a wide variety of life experiences- had to develop strategies to deal with love and its challenges. These strategies were not only used to improve on how the AJ interacted with the opposite sex, but to also help him to effectively deal with the intricacies of the individual and collective interactions with these women; whenever he became an adult.

## Dealing with love and its challenges-as the adult

There came a time in the life of the AJ that he was in a better position to handle the pressures of the opposite sex than that which he encountered as a teenager. The AJ was also better able to handle these pressures without the need to hide the effects of the many advances from his parents. Why was that so? The reason was that the AJ became an adult.

Dealing with love and its challenges did not get any less as the AJ became an adult. In fact, the interpersonal relationship situations became more intricate for the AJ in that, there were occasions when the he had to 'save some of these ladies from themselves'. What does that mean? How weird was that for the AJ? The AJ presented at least two scenarios in this book to illustrate/ explain why he used the above mentioned phrase.

In understanding the circumstances of the first scenario, the AJ supposed that you were enjoying a healthy loving relationship with your partner. In this relationship, your wife has provided you with all the food, nourishment, attention, love and care that you ever desire. However, as soon as your wife went away from you-even for a short time- your female neighbor brought you more food, nourishment, attention, love and care; often without your expressed request of her to do. What would you do?

Well, essence of this scenario happened to the AJ. On that fateful day in his young adult life, the AJ explained that he and his girlfriend at the time had just had an erotic sexual experience. Soon thereafter, she left for her home. About 10 minutes later, while doing household chores in the kitchen, the AJ received an unexpected female visitor (who he had not seen for approximately 6 years). The AJ invited her sit in the living room for a moment until he had completed his kitchen chores.

The AJ completed his chores, and then returned to the living room, in order to begin entertaining the unexpected female guest; only to enter an empty room! To his amazement, the AJ noticed that she not only left in the living room, but she was in one of the bedrooms- 'stark naked'. As soon as the AJ entered the entrance to the bedroom, this female mounted the bed in anticipation for action.

It was then that the AJ posited the tenets of the scenario mentioned earlier to her. She told the AJ that she felt 'kind of cute' about the situation, but she was insistent that she wanted to have sex with him; despite his hinting to the contrary. After reluctantly preparing to comply with her wishes, on observation of his parts, she hurriedly grabbed her clothing and sprinted out of his house. Yikes!

The AJ never saw this female again until about 7 years later. At this meeting, she indicated that she got married a few years after her encounter with the AJ- with two children.

At this point, the AJ posited another scenario indicating how he had to 'save another woman from herself'. The AJ met another woman while working at an establishment who - from her behavior- showed that she liked him very much. Eventually, a relationship was developed between the AJ and this woman.

During the interactions, the AJ not only discovered that she was already in a relationship with another fellow (of approximately 2 years), but this man was also supporting her financially. In addition, this woman told the AJ that she always spoke fondly of him to this fellow, while she hardly mentioned anything about him to the AJ whenever they were together. Yikes! It got weirder for the AJ to handle.

Incidentally, this woman wanted to have sex with the AJ, but felt obliged to the other fellow. (Ooh, she was a virgin at that time.) On that fateful day, while she was visiting the home of the AJ, she not only wanted to have sex with him there, but she was still confused about the obligations of the other fellow in her life. In fact, this woman was prepared to have sex with the AJ and the other man at a later date; in order to decide which one of the men she should choose to settle down with.

On discovery of her dilemma, the AJ told her to forget about him, and focus on the other fellow. In addition, the AJ showed her that given the situation, the other guy (who knew of the AJ) would wish of the opportunity to destroy her sexually, and then he would 'dump' her. The AJ did not have sex with her that day (or ever). He ushered her out of his house, and sent her back to her fate with the other guy; or whomever else she chose. The AJ never saw this woman ever again.

At this point, the AJ would like to mention another weird discovery that he had to deal with, pertaining to the interactions with women who 'graced' his life and made his life worth living. He found out that he may have the dubious distinction of being intimately involved with women who never wanted their intimate relationship with him to end, ever. These women were unconcerned with whether time had elapsed, or the situations/circumstances have changed. As long as he is alive, there seemed to be enough hope for them (these women) to want to re-kindle the good times they had with him; irrespective of whether he is currently intimately involved with another woman at the time as his partner/girlfriend/wife.

Given the reality mentioned above, the AJ had to learn how to deal with other weirdly related events that have occurred when he interacted with ladies, such as (a) how to handle multiple female clashes over him, and/or (b) how to handle abnormal situations concerning his ex-girl friends and/or with other women (some of whom he had never had an acquaintance with, ever). Having highlighted two of the many scenarios surrounding the weird discovery about his life and love life situations, the AJ shall recall some of them to you the reader.

Firstly, the AJ has had to continually deal with many clashes involving at least one of his ex-girlfriends and his current lady/partner in his life. For example, he had to deal with a situation where six of his ex-girlfriends visited him unexpectedly, at his home, many years ago. At the time, the AJ was a young adult, living with his dad. Each of these women not only appeared at the AJ's gate at a few minutes interval apart, but each of them wanted to discuss different matters with him. Please note, all of these women visited the home 'unannounced' and without prior notification.

Fortunately for the AJ, he was able to place each of these

ex-girlfriend visitors at different locations in the yard, so that each of them could get some privacy in order to have their individual issues addressed. Interestingly, while each of these six ex-girlfriends was being strategically placed in the yard- to ensure their privacy- the bona fide girlfriend (at the time) also visited him at his house. The AJ not only ensured that the bona fide girlfriend (at the time) was afforded her respectful position by escorting her inside the house, but he also allowed her to be comfortably catered for, until he could attend to her personally.

One of the ex-girlfriends voiced her objection to the AJ about the type of treatment that was given to the bona fide girlfriend, when compared to hers. The AJ had to gently remind her that she was, and the bona fide girlfriend is.

Of course, each clash situation had to be addressed using innovative methods. For example, there was an occasion when the behavior of a female friend caused an 'unfortunate' situation to occur in the life of the AJ. As a result, he had to put stringent measures in place, in order to adequately deal with the situation. The impact of the approaches employed by the AJ to tackle the unfortunate situation and the disobedience of this female friend caused her to 'cross paths' with him. The situation became very explosive, to the extent that the authorities were called in to sort it out promptly.

Soon afterwards, this said young lady subsequently told the AJ that despite the circumstances, the 'hatchet was buried' by her, and all sources of contention were addressed amicably. She has also requested that normalcy of the relationship between the both parties should be maintained, with urgency. How weird could that get for the AJ?

If you thought that the incidents mentioned earlier were weird, wait until you read of this next situation. Here goes.

A few years ago, the AJ and his girlfriend at the time, were sleeping in one of the beds in his home (of the multi-bed room house). At about 12:45am, the AJ was awakened by a sound of someone tapping very softly – almost intimately- on his window. He sprang up out of bed and looked through the top window; only to see a very pretty, well contoured, properly clad young lady standing outside the window.

The AJ asked her why was she standing at his window; to which she began asking him for some money so that she could use it to help her to care for child. The AJ wondered what could cause this lovely young lady to be asking him such a question, at this time of the morning. Worse of all, he did not know the woman!

At that point, the AJ not only declined her monetary request, but he also ordered her to go through his gate and leave his premises. This lady then asked for a specific monetary denominational amount. Once again, this request was declined by the AJ. On his insistence, the young lady eventually obeyed him and left his home. On her departure, (while going through the gate) she said goodbye in a loud voice-which could wake up the neighbors at that time of the morning- jumped into her car and drove off into the darkness.

Of note, throughout the verbal exchanges between the AJ and the strange 'early morning' female visitor were heard by his girlfriend; who was sharing the same bed with the AJ at the time. After dismissing the unknown woman from the house, without opening the window or offering to open the front door in order to accommodate the presence of strange female visitor, the AJ's girlfriend at the time only said "Mmm, such a request at this time of night?", and went back to bed.

How weird could that get for the AJ? Imagine for a moment, how things could have changed dramatically if the AJ had either; (a) opened the window in order to speak with the female visitor or, (b) gotten out of bed to open the front door in order to engage this woman in further conversation? If the AJ had done any of the two things, he could not convince his girlfriend at the time, or anyone else that he has not been entertaining and disposing of his female guests in a similar fashion, at various times of the morning. In addition, the AJ could not convince his girlfriend (at the time) that that he has been innocent of such a claim of doing same, in her absence (that is whenever when did not stay over until in the morning). Yikes!

On a different note, the main encounter that the AJ had with gunmen occurred as a result of visiting his girlfriends. The AJ was held up by a gunman at a lonely spot in the bushes close to a bridge located nearby his home. This event took place at about 1:00am, after visiting two of my girlfriends who lived in the same area. He was robbed of approximately $100.00, and released. To date, these women have not been told of this ordeal as yet.

In dealing with love and its challenges, the AJ had not been spared of the need to make tough decisions; all of which usually have accompanied with the requisite consequences. This activity ought to be expected in all love relationships between man and woman. In the case of the AJ, he had to do things to protect himself from the women who feel that if they cannot have him (at all cost) then nobody else shall be allowed to do same.

Interestingly, many women have told the AJ –especially those who have already had an intimate relationship with him in the past- that they would openly create his demise, should the intimate relationship end. In this case, the AJ had reason to end a relationship with one of his girlfriends at the time. Soon afterwards, he overheard her discussing her intention to do bodily harm to him by using an implement that she was making arrangement to obtain for herself. Having heard the contents of the conversation, he intercepted it, and the authorities were called in. The authorities were able to effect rectifying measures that provided a deterrent to her thoughts and possible collaboration activities being contemplated. Wow!

Indeed, based on the many experiences that the AJ has been involved with, he has had reasons to think why several weird outcomes have occurred between many of the women who entered a love (sexual) relationship with him. The AJ thought that many of these women, who entered into such arrangements of love and intimacy, may have done so with a weakened chance of having a long lasting relationship.

As a reminder, the AJ' has already thought that the strength of any love relationship shall be dependent on a number of attributes. These attributes could be: (a) the socialization of both parties; (b) ones own skill set of endowments; (c) the willingness of both parties to depart from carrying any 'baggage' into the current relationship; (d) the collective strength of character of both individuals, and; (e) the impact of both families and friends on the relationship; both with respect to the psyche of the individuals and their behavior towards each other in the relationship.

Without using the correct attributes mentioned above, often, the relationship shall be affected by the casualties of events that, if not corrected on a timely basis, could ultimately lead to the demise of the love relationship.

As time passed, in each of these situations, the AJ has conducted a self induced pre-and post evaluation of the demise of the relationships that he had been in. He has concluded that several of the women had carried 'baggage' from previous love/life/ sexual interpersonal experiences; which were not adequately addressed prior to, or during the lifetime of the relationship.

As a result of not dealing with the 'baggage' issue in a proper way, this situation often lead to problems - that were eventually unresolved – culminating to the ending of the relationship. For example, at least one of the women who were part of a failed love relationship with the AJ admitted that she did individual/collective control. For example, while studying in Asia, the AJ has been fortunate to become intimately involved in a relationship with a woman; of a different creed and ethnic origin. This young lady resided in a 'land locked' nation there in Asia. Interestingly, this country seldom saw black people living or visiting there.

Despite, great intentions, it would have been very challenging for either of the two parties to move and live in each other country. Also, it was be difficult for the AJ to be accepted as a part of her family. Hence, the relationship between this Asian woman and the AJ actually 'died' its natural death, when both parties returned to their respective native homeland.

At this point, one may wonder if the AJ's sporting life has influenced his love relationship with women in any way possible. Interestingly, there were cases when the love relationships between both parties evolved over time because many of these girls/ women were not only physically and emotionally attracted to a high performance sportsman like the AJ, but the reverse situation also held true for both groups of persons. Naturally, the mutual benefits of sharing love and sexual relations were received between the AJ and these 'groupie' women.

Suffice it to say that the AJ met his (then) wife as a result of playing competitive volleyball; while attending/ studying at University. Ooh, his marriage lasted less than two years and it ended in divorce, a few years later. All was not lost during that experience, as it was during the AJ's marriage that his sweet 'puddytat' daughter was born. Of course, that was a delightful moment in the life of the AJ.

In summary, it was expected that some men may have experienced some of the events similar to the AJ. However, it would be more interesting to note if many of these persons were privileged to state categorically that they experienced all of the collective things, as did the AJ. Could these individuals say that their collective experiences affected their respective love relationships in a similar way as that of the AJ? Perhaps, the answer to that question has been obvious. Also, do you think that the AJ can stop wondering how weird it got for him, as it related to his love relationship with women?

## The AJ- simmering like a meal cooking in a pot

The AJ has taken note of the frequency, magnitude, and variety of life experiences that he has had, over time. In that light, the AJ often wondered what life lessons have been learnt by him so far. Many persons have not only approached the AJ seeking information and guidance on several topics, but several of them have been amazed about his feats. These persons usually exclaim how could the AJ - of ordinary means – experience so many different, complex situations in his lifetime, yet he could remain 'unassuming' in nature. The AJ thought that perhaps, his greatest life lessons have caused him to develop the unique skill sets, allowing him to simmer! Ooh yes, the AJ has learnt how to simmer.

Remember that whenever a cook has decided to make a meal simmer, the cook already knew that this meal has been over 95 percent cooked. In simmering, the meal has been given a few more minutes to allow the steam in the pot to enhance the quality of the finished product by (a) either loosing a bit more fluid or, (b) gaining more stock. In the end, (after the simmering exercise) the meal usually became almost perfectly tasty and delicious for human consumption. How could such a description (of simmering) fit the profile of someone like the AJ?

The AJ - being full of energy, vigor and enterprise- he thought he could use his unique skill in such a way that, in the end, the world would be a better place to live in. However, the hierarchy not only had different ideas about that thought, but they often have implemented several strategies to counteract it. Could you believe that? The AJ has had many reasons to think that the 'power brokers' in the hierarchy of the schema of things have tried to ensure that the influence of the AJ was stymied. In fact, attempts have been made by these persons (groups of persons) to 'put a lid' on his influence on the world; with limited success.

Interestingly, the AJ has discovered that despite acknowledging that the 'lid on his pot of life' was already in place, he has learnt how to allow himself to have controlled periodic releases of his energies, expertise, and enterprise to the benefit to the society. Also, the product of the AJ's 'pot of life' could be likened to the preparation of a properly cooked meal. Therefore, in simmering, the AJ thought that he was enhancing the purity, taste and quality of his product; without the unnecessary 'spilling' of the contents over the 'rim of his pot of life'.

At this point, the AJ has compiled a few thoughts of reflection on the impact of his many and varied life experiences on (a) the development of his pertinent life lessons, and (b) the quality of life that he has enjoyed so far.

Please note that this shortlist of life lessons were not compiled based on the order of importance. Firstly, the AJ recognized that not everyone will accept his point of view on any topic, even if it can be proven that his opinion on the topic should to be the correct position /point of view to be adopted.

Secondly, despite his enthusiasm (knowledge and expertise), the AJ has to exercise tolerance and patience in most situations, even if it can be proven that his approach at dealing with these situations can be validated (and others have malicious intentions).

Thirdly, the AJ has learnt how to avoid confrontations, even though there were times when confrontations are unavoidable. He chose to defer to this position especially when his approach at dealing with the issues can be proven to be morally, intellectually, psychologically and practically correct.

Fourthly, the AJ has to try to work with detractors, especially when these persons are placed in a higher position than he, in the hierarchy of command/ influence in the schema of things.

Fifthly, the AJ has decided not to waiver on his principles. However, he has learnt how to temper his delivery, especially when the persons reacting to, and understanding the issues were predicated on their socialization, limited experiences, exposure and so on.

Sixthly, in any situation, the AJ has learnt when to 'shut up' and 'walk away'. Often, because of his unique attributes (such as having a complex personality, clarity of thought, and son on) several persons-especially of a lesser disposition-often object to almost anything that he proposes, in any forum. The AJ accepted that even with prompting, he needed to learn to exercise self control and 'shut up' and/ or 'walk away from the circumstances that currently exist.

Seventhly, the AJ has many 'outlets' to re-channel his energies. He has also been aware that others outside of the current forum/gathering that he presided over may be more receptive to his ideas/ contributions than that he has presented to his current audience. In that light, he has the ability and the audience to re-route his energies/efforts to these outlets; knowing that these persons often show greater appreciation of his input towards the betterment of their lives, than that of the original audience.

Eight of all, the zeal that the AJ has to do good for humanity cannot be swayed or derailed by other persons or circumstances. Therefore, just like a cook who chose to allow a meal in a pot to simmer, in the end, as in the case of the AJ, the expectations and final outcome usually coincide; as being the best outcome for him and the society. In addition, controlled releases of 'steam' from his 'pot of life' often lead to improvements of his product, over time

Ninthly, it has often occurred when the AJ has to fight for what should be rightfully his. Although the battles may seem tough, he not only usually prevailed over time, often vindicating his original position on the subject, but the successes were noted despite the efforts of the detractors (who want to stifle the truth from being known to others).

Finally, the AJ can state that the amassing of power usually has been synonymous with him, yet he did not seek it for himself. He preferred to share the power than hoard it; as in sharing, this action usually strengthens the authenticity of the AJ in the world. Given these realities, he has no need to crave the power or to control 'the seat of power'. How weird could this get?

Clearly, the AJ has used the many life lessons learnt (such as those listed above and the many others that were not included in this book) to enhance the quality of his life on earth. As a result, he has been able to fully appreciate the benefits of living freely, in an atmosphere of complexities and challenges.

Interestingly, the AJ has often indicated to all persons he interacted with that he always advocated for open expressions of the truth to be presented at all times, for all mankind to see and enjoy the benefits thereof. As a result, the AJ has discovered that people (especially of the opposite sex) continue to befriend him. He has often stated that he has no need to prove anything about his character to anyone; as the proof of whatever he advocated have not been hidden from anyone. Hence, he can afford to 'simmer' and still enjoy the high quality lifestyle that he has chosen for himself; without the stresses that could be associated with living.

www.ingramcontent.com/pod-product-compliance
Lightning Source LLC
Chambersburg PA
CBHW061248040426
42444CB00010B/2296